Last Chapter
and WOrse

Other Books in The Far Side Series

The Far Side
Beyond The Far Side
In Search of The Far Side
Bride of The Far Side
Valley of The Far Side
It Came From The Far Side
Hound of The Far Side
The Far Side Observer
Night of the Crash-Test Dummies
Wildlife Preserves
Wiener Dog Art
Unnatural Selections
Cows of Our Planet
The Chickens Are Restless
The Curse of Madame "C"

Anthologies

The Far Side Gallery
The Far Side Gallery 2
The Far Side Gallery 3
The Far Side Gallery 4
The Far Side Gallery 5

Retrospective

The PreHistory of The Far Side: A 10th Anniversary Exhibit

a FAR SIDe COLLECTIOn

Last Chapter
and WOrse

bby
GAry Lars●n

Andrews and McMeeL
A UNiversal Press Syndicate C●mpany
KAnsas City

Library of Congress Catalog Card: 96-83997

ISBN: 0-8362-2131-1

Printed on recycled paper.

Last Chapter

Here are the cartoons taken from my final six months of newspaper syndication, plus 13 new cartoons I drew since I retired (more about that on page 81). Mingled with these are a few other cartoons that were never published in a Far Side book. (I know there are three guys out there who are tracking this stuff.)

But *Last Chapter and Worse,* I should hasten to add, is not necessarily my last "gasp" in the cartooning world. The Call of the Vial (of ink) still speaks to me, and the thought of creating more mischief—somewhere, sometime—still rumbles in the reptilian complex of my brain. (For you non-biology types, we've all got that—it ain't just me.)

My most profound thanks to all of you who have shared my sense of humor while forgiving my foibles. If I managed to give you a few laughs or smiles or gag reflexes along the way, you've given me a wonderful and completely unforeseen career.

I hope to see you again one day.

—*Gary Larson*

"CHICKEN UP!"

"There he goes again. ... Satan's pet."

It was over. But the way the townsfolk called it,
neither man was a clear winner.

"JOHNSON! BACK IN FORMATION! ... Dang,
I hate sidewinders."

Until God warned him to knock it off, Noah would often try to get a little poker game going with some of the dumb animals.

In ancient Rome, it was tough for the guys who worked in the vomitoriums to get dates.

"Well, it *was* a private table."

Understanding only German, Fritz was unaware
that the clouds were becoming threatening.

This time, his practical jokes had gone too far,
and Wally was finally booted off the hill.

"The problem, Mr. Fudd, is that you've been having a subliminal effect on everyone in the factory. We're proud of our product, Mr. Fudd, and there's no company in the world that builds a finer skwoo dwivuh. ... Dang! Now you got me doing it!"

"OK, you two! Problem solved!"

After years of harboring his secret desires,
Ned finally hits on the senior librarian.

By secretly working out for many months, Irwin
became the envy of all the 98-pound weaklings.

"But on the other hand, Feldman, having the biggest brain among us means that it is mere child's play to subdue you with an ordinary headlock!"

At the Grizzly Ball, only Alice, with her kind heart, would not refuse to dance with Adams.

At the Cowboy Wax Museum

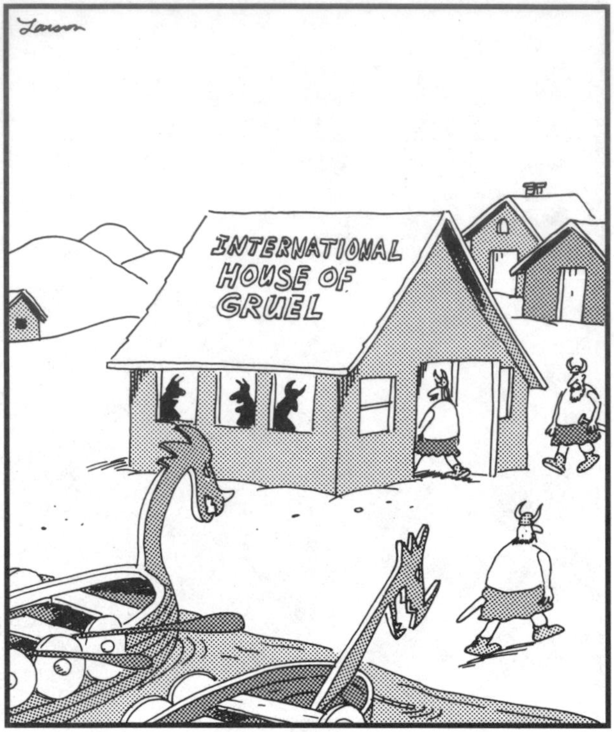
Larson
INTERNATIONAL HOUSE OF GRUEL

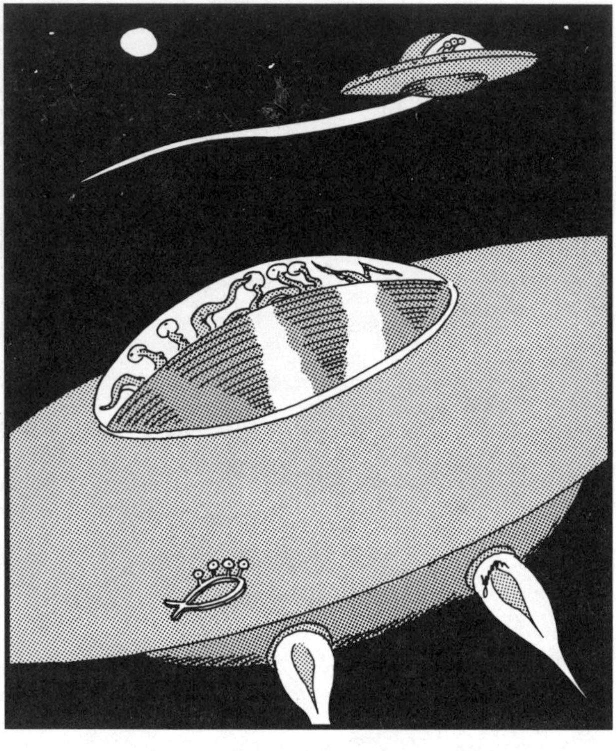

"OK, let's start the exam. Stinking caps on,
everyone—stinking caps on."

The life and times of Captain Hazelwood

The curse of mad scientist's block

"Look. You *had* five bones, right? Your friend Zooky comes over, stays awhile, then leaves. *Now* you have *four* bones, right? ... You don't have to be a 'Lassie' to figure this one out."

"Don't eat the flippers, Zeke,
or they'll know we're tourists."

"No way was it me, Mom—you must've
heard a peep out of Eddie."

"You're up, Red."

Hellbillies

Once again, a meeting between management and the
Plutonium Truckers' Union grows tense.

"I'm leaving you, Mitchell. You've never
had tunnel vision; you never will."

Lacking a horse, Jed was compelled to just drift
along with the tumbling tumbleweed.

"Well, Griselda's back from the plastic surgeon's. ...
Whoa! Look at the size of that wart!"

"Excuse me, Captain, but while we're waiting, would you like to join the crew and myself for a little snorkeling?"

"Situation's changed, Jules. ... Take my buffalo gun and hand me my mime rifle."

"I'm afraid you misunderstood. ... I said
I'd like a mango."

"Whoa! Here we go again! ... 'Pony Express
Rider Walks into Workplace, Starts
Shooting Every Horse in Sight.'"

Big dogs having fun with helium

When the dust had settled, a lone figure was revealed standing on the small knoll. Yes, he, too, was a herd animal—but he was *through* runnin'.

"Oh, they'll find something for you real soon. ... Me?
I'm forever blowing bubbles."

"I make no claims about all my success, Bernard.
I never went to school, I never worked hard,
and I'm not particularly bright. ... I'm just a
lucky skunk, Bernard."

"Convertible! Convertible!"

Marv remained calm. No matter how thoroughly
they searched, the agents never discovered
his "secret" pocket.

Scene from *Dog Invaders from Mars.*

Stand-semierect comedy

Bunker Hill, June 17, 1775: An unfortunate twist of fate for one young Redcoat, Charles "Bugeyed" Dingham, was not knowing that the opposing American general had just uttered the historic command, "Don't fire until you see the whites of their eyes."

In their final year, all research science students
are required to take one semester
of Maniacal Laughter.

"Sorry, Bobby, but you know the rule—no swimming for a week after eating."

"Oh, Helen! You're pregnant? That's wonderful! ... At first, I was taking you quite literally when you said you had one in the oven."

31

"Ok, that's pretty good! ... Now! I want everyone on this side of the aisle to come in rubbing their legs together when I signal! ... And let's show the other side how it's done!"

"Boy, you wiped out, Kumba. ... Nothing left but rebar."

By simply attaching the new ACME Wingbaby,
airlines can significantly improve their
passengers' overall comfort.

"Well, first you say you saw the defendant at the scene and now you say you *think* you saw him! ... Let's cut to the chase, Ms. Sunbeam—is it possible your entire testimony is nothing more than a mere fairy tale?"

Every Saturday morning, while his playmates patiently waited, little Normy Bates would always take a few extra minutes to yell at his "dog."

The often romanticized image of cowboys and aliens

"There're some, folks! These rare and lovely creations have no natural enemies, but balloon animals never last too long in this harsh land."

"Waiter! What's that soup doin' on my fly?"

Scene from *Fiddle Attraction*

"Hell, Ben, you catch a few bullets through your hat during *every* holdup, and I'm finally gonna say I ain't ever been much impressed."

Dogs and alcohol: The tragic untold story.

"That's just not impressive, Doris. ... The brain!
Hold up the big brain!"

"And the note says: 'Dear classmates and Ms. Kilgore:
Now that my family has moved away, I feel bad that
I whined so much about being mistreated. Hope
the contents of this box will set things right.
Love, Pandora.' ... How sweet."

"I'm starting to worry about you, Earl. ... Stalking
sheep in that outfit is one thing, but wearing it
around the house is just a little kinky."

"I might have missed, Lou, but I take some satisfaction
in knowing I busted up their little party."

Life in the Old Weth

Artist: G. Larson
Medium: Ink on paper
Title: It Was Late and I Was Tired

The ultimate gopher insult

"One day, Wilson, *I'll* be sitting at that desk."

"And I say we go outside and we *play with this ball!*"

"Oh, yeah! They work real hard, all day long,
seven days a week! ... And here's the
best part—*for chicken feed!*"

The Army's last-ditch effort to destroy Mothra.

Drawn by the pulsating sound of a rock thumping on a dead armadillo, two Australopithecines stood at the forest edge. Instantly, Thog's agent knew they had a crossover hit.

Slave-ship daily schedules

"I know you miss the Wainwrights, Bobby, but they were weak and stupid people—and that's why we have wolves and other large predators."

"Hey hey hey! ... Before you go, pack up this depressing garbage of yours and get it out of here!"

"Everyone just keep their nets real still. ... They'll
just want to look over our jars, and we
best not try to stop them."

"I'm sorry, Delores, I didn't think you'd truly
ever leave! ... But where will you go?"

"But before we begin, this announcement: Mr. Johnson! Mr. Frank Johnson! ... If you're out there, the conference organizers would like you to know that you were never actually invited."

Despite his repeated efforts to explain things to her, Satan could never dissuade his mother from offering cookies and milk to the accursed.

On monster refrigerators

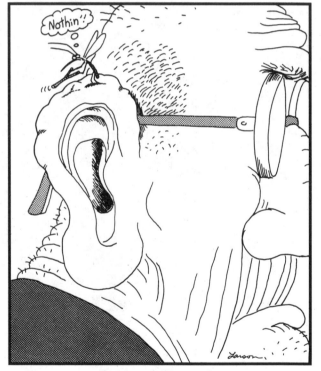

Insect witching rods

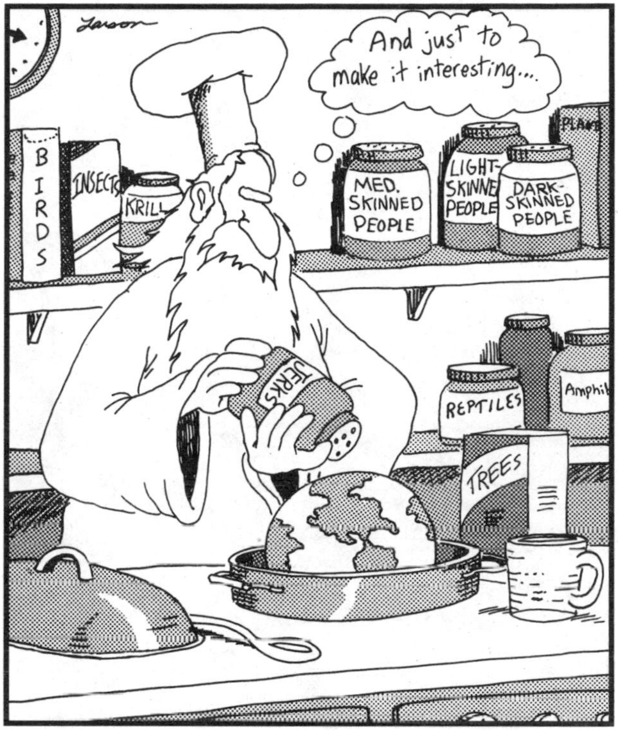
And just to make it interesting....
BIRDS
INSECTS
KRILL
MED. SKINNED PEOPLE
DARK-SKINNED PEOPLE
JERKS
REPTILES
TREES

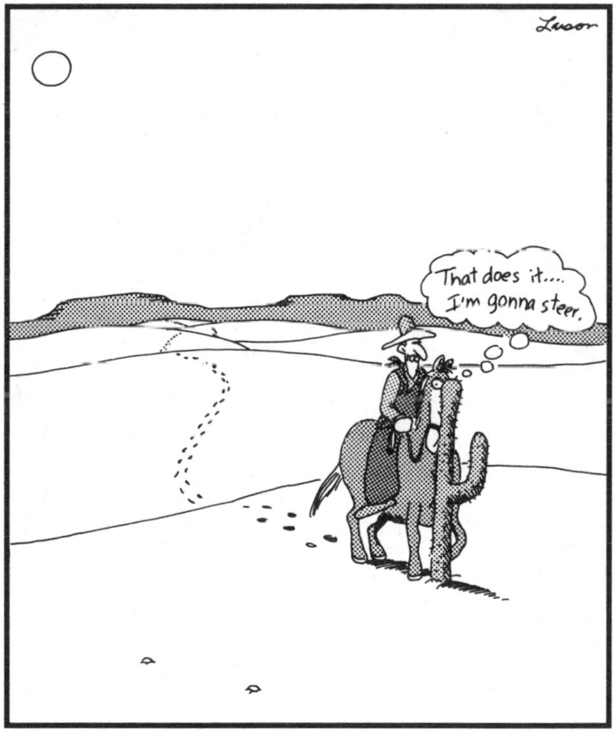
That does it.... I'm gonna steer.

"Oh my gosh! You know what that is, Mooky? ... My dad had one when I was a kid!"

Marie Antoinette's last-ditch effort to save her head.

"Excuse me? *Excuse* me? ... I believe the biggest set of fang marks belong to *me*, my friend!"

Your typical beeswax lunch

"Well, lad, you caught me fair and square. ... But truthfully, as far as leprechauns go, I've never been considered all that lucky."

Sheep authors

Executioner understudies

"Anybody else? ... This here's a school for *buffalo* hunters—and anyone who so much as *utters* the word 'bison' can join Morgenstern in the corner!"

At the Crabbiness Research Institute

"Say. ... It's only a paper moon."

As Myles left the safari club, his stomach suddenly knotted up. Foolishly, he had ignored the warnings not to park his Land Rover in this part of Tanzania.

"You folks like flies? Well, wait 'til you see the parlor!"

"Leonard painted that and hung it up just this afternoon. ... He calls it, 'It's *My* Couch! *My* Couch! Don't They Understand?'"

An unnatural silence hung in the kitchen, and Spunky sensed that his arrival was unexpected.

"You're darn lucky, Saunders. ... If that rhino had really respected you as an enemy, he'd have done a heck of a lot more than just slap your face."

Zorg dupes the entire tribe in an incident later
known in prehistory books as "firegate."

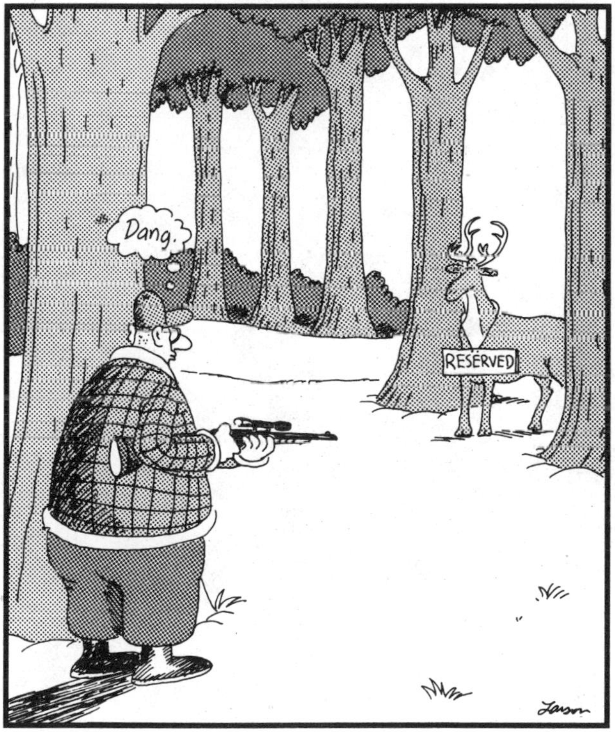
Dang.
RESERVED
Larson

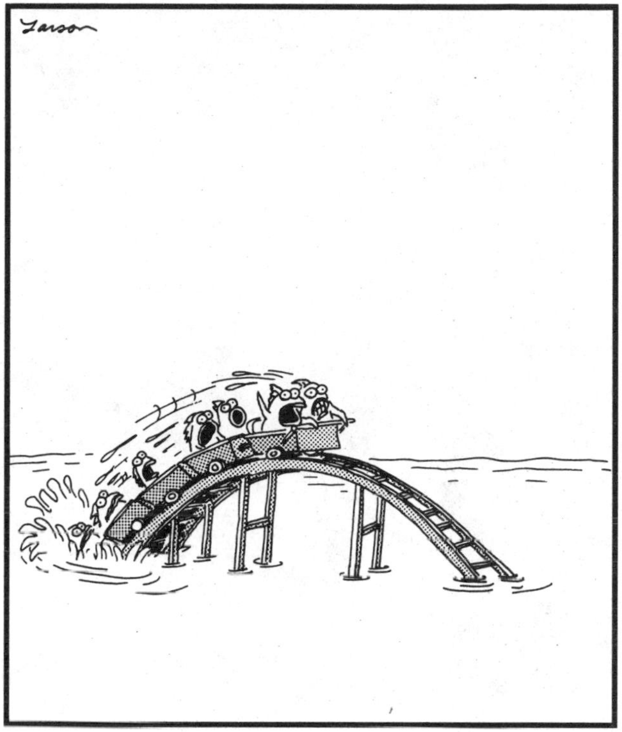
Larson

Fish rides

"He's making his nest now. ... There! See it?
That son-of-a- ... he's got himself a futon!"

"Whoa whoa whoa! ... You'll have to go
back and walk through again."

"And yes, Norman *was* beheaded, cleaned, and plucked. ... But we all know Norman's wacky sense of humor, and we can take comfort knowing he would've gotten a kick out of this."

Throughout their songwriting careers, the Gershwins rarely discussed their younger brother, Nathan, who played gutbucket.

"Well, hell no, I can't tell Harriet! ... First thing she's gonna ask me is what was I doin' checkin' out a decoy!"

"Uh, uh, uh—I wouldn't do that, Thorg. I know how to use this thing."

"Now what theorem applies to this ... Douglas!
Is that a fly you're sucking on? Well, I hope
you brought enough for everyone!"

Hunting lodge readings

"OK, here's one, Marv: What's got 12 legs, six eyes,
a hairy thorax, was found dead in its display
case this morning, and goes 'crunch'
inside a submarine sandwich?"

In the longest hour of his life, Morty takes the dare
of his sloth buddies and crosses the autobahn.

Abdul flunks

In its more horrific method of retribution, the mob will sometimes dress victims as mimes, place them in glass boxes, and let them perish slowly in full view of the public.

"Well, it came from your division, Sanders, and as you can see, it's covered with honey and molasses! ... You know what that makes this, Sanders!"

"Everyone can just put down their loot and plunder, and Sven here—yes, old Sven, who was in charge of reading the tide chart—has something to say to us all."

"You ever get that urge, Frank? It begins with looking down from 50 stories up, thinking about the meaninglessness of life, listening to dark voices deep inside you, and you think, 'Should I? ... Should I? ... Should I push someone off?'"

"We're *not* going to the mountains, so shut up and let's go! ... Most kids would count their lucky stars that every vacation their folks took 'em to the beach!"

"And so, as you enter the adult phase of your life, you will thank God that these past 17 years of being stuck in the ground and unable to move are over. ... Congratulations, cicadas of '94!"

"Remo! Lift with your knees, not your back!"

"Yeah, I just got back! And the wizard I mentioned? He gave me a new brain! ... It's on the coffee table as we speak!"

The gods play with Ted and Jerry

"Your dog had both motive and opportunity, ma'am: He hated the cat and he's had training in operating heavy machinery. ... Your husband, we feel, was just in the wrong place at the wrong time."

"And *you*! What's *your* story? ... If you ain't a mutineer, then what the hell are you?"

"You know, sometimes I sort of enjoy this herd mentality."

"The *first* thing I'm gonna do is wipe that smile off your face!"

"Sorry, Virgil—that's all you get. ... I don't know how you got hold of a dribble glass in the first place, but it's just your bad luck."

"It's worse than I first suspected, Mr. Binkley—you don't even *have* a funny bone."

"Hey! Hey! Hey! ... Who's the wiseguy that
just turned down the thermostat?"

"Look, marriage is OK—but I also want my own identity. ... I mean, how would *you* like it if everyone referred to *you* as 'Chocolate Bar and Chocolate Bar'?"

"It's no good, Dawson! We're being sucked in by the sun's gravitational field and there's nothing we can do! ... And let me add those are my sunglasses you're wearing!"

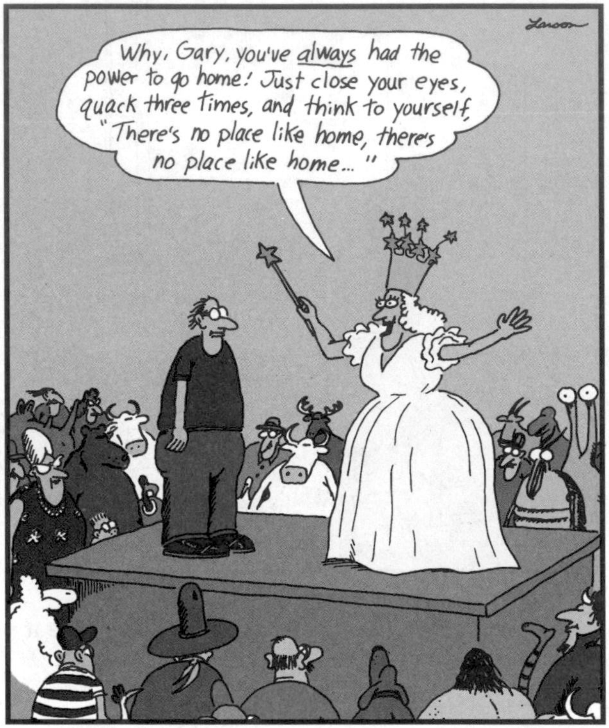
Larson
Why, Gary, you've always had the power to go home! Just close your eyes, quack three times, and think to yourself, "There's no place like home, there's no place like home..."

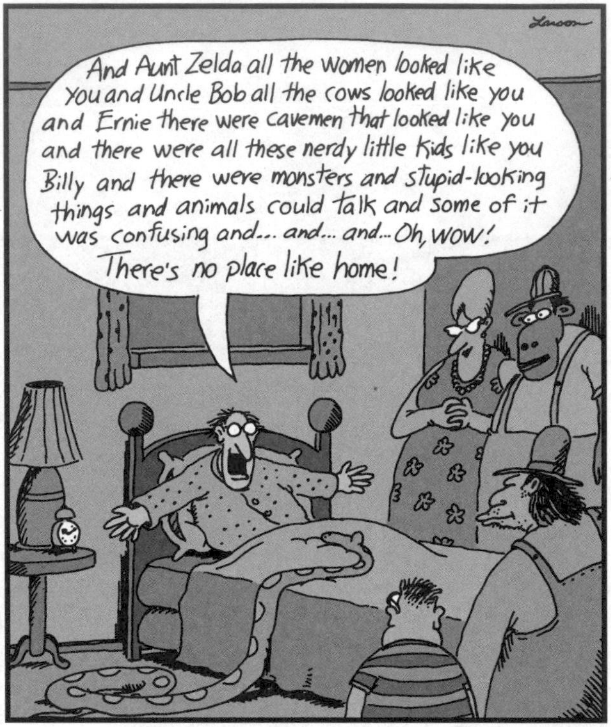
Larson
And Aunt Zelda all the women looked like you and Uncle Bob all the cows looked like you and Ernie there were cavemen that looked like you and there were all these nerdy little kids like you Billy and there were monsters and stupid-looking things and animals could talk and some of it was confusing and... and... and... Oh, WOW! There's no place like home!

... And Worse

When the cartoons for this book were being compiled, my editor called me up and said, "Uh, Gary—we're thirteen short." I've never been exactly sure how the number of cartoons that must constitute a book was ever determined, but someone apparently knows the rule. (Personally, I've always lobbied for between fourteen and twenty.)

Anyway, a year after my retirement, I did sit back down at the drawing table for a couple of weeks and developed thirteen cartoons (a fitting number, I suppose) that previously have never seen the light of day. I say "developed," because most of what follows I had already doodled in my sketch book at the time of my retirement, and a couple others were nixed ideas for book covers (pages 89 and 101).

So, if you thought of *The Far Side* as a refrigerator, here are some things that were growing way in the back. Don't eat them.

When dumb animals attempt murder.

"It's just a simple Rorschach ink-blot test, Mr. Bromwell, so just calm down and tell me what each one suggests to you."

"Well, I suppose it'll be a few thousand more years before
we get an 'Arts and Leisure' section."

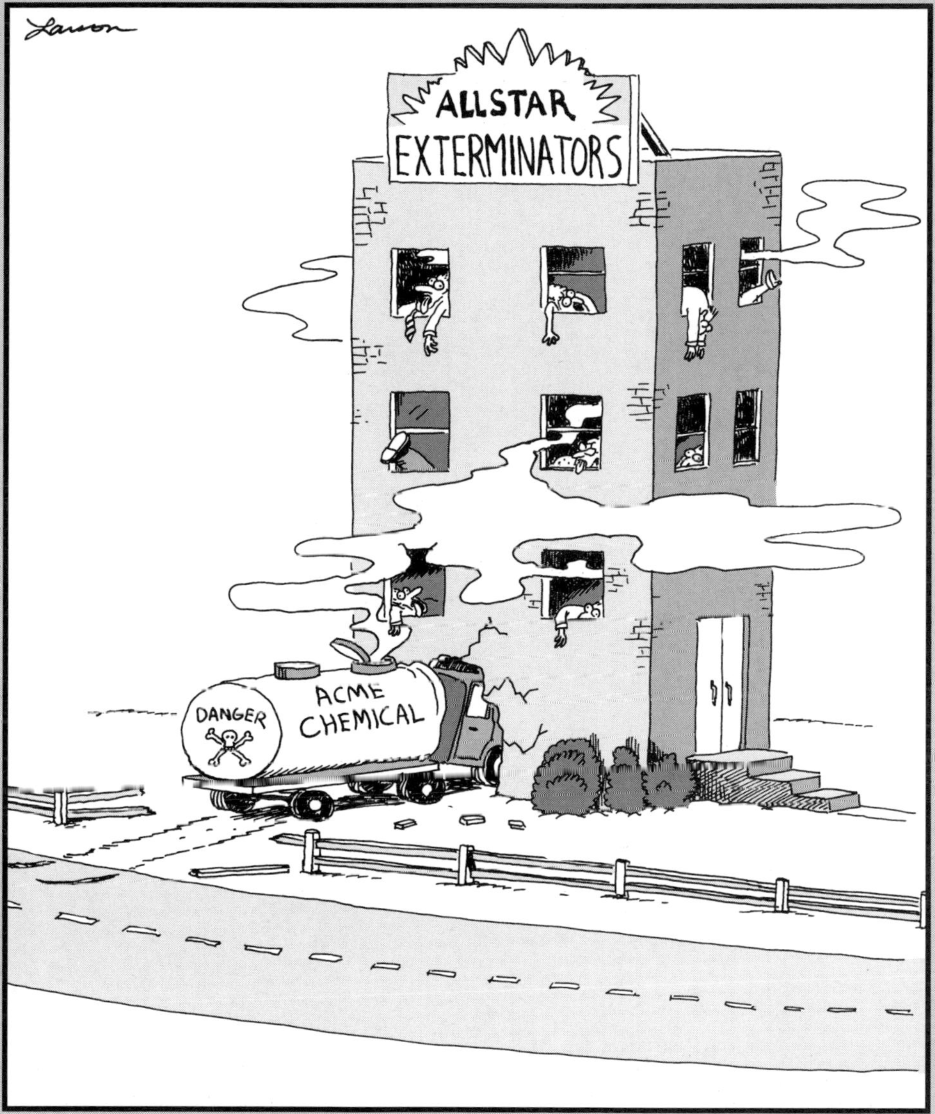
Larson
ALLSTAR
EXTERMINATORS
DANGER
ACME
CHEMICAL

"Yeah, he's good—but there was an orangutan
in here last week that could *bury* him!"

"Hey Frank ... nice and cool here in the shade ... yesiree ... niiiiice and cool."

"You know, Ned, you're my best friend, and I just gotta tell someone.
It's time I come out of the closet and stop living this lie. ... I hate animals."

"I've been looking at your time sheets, Webster ... leaving early, coming in late, etc., etc. ...Working for the railroad, Webster, means working *all* the live long day."

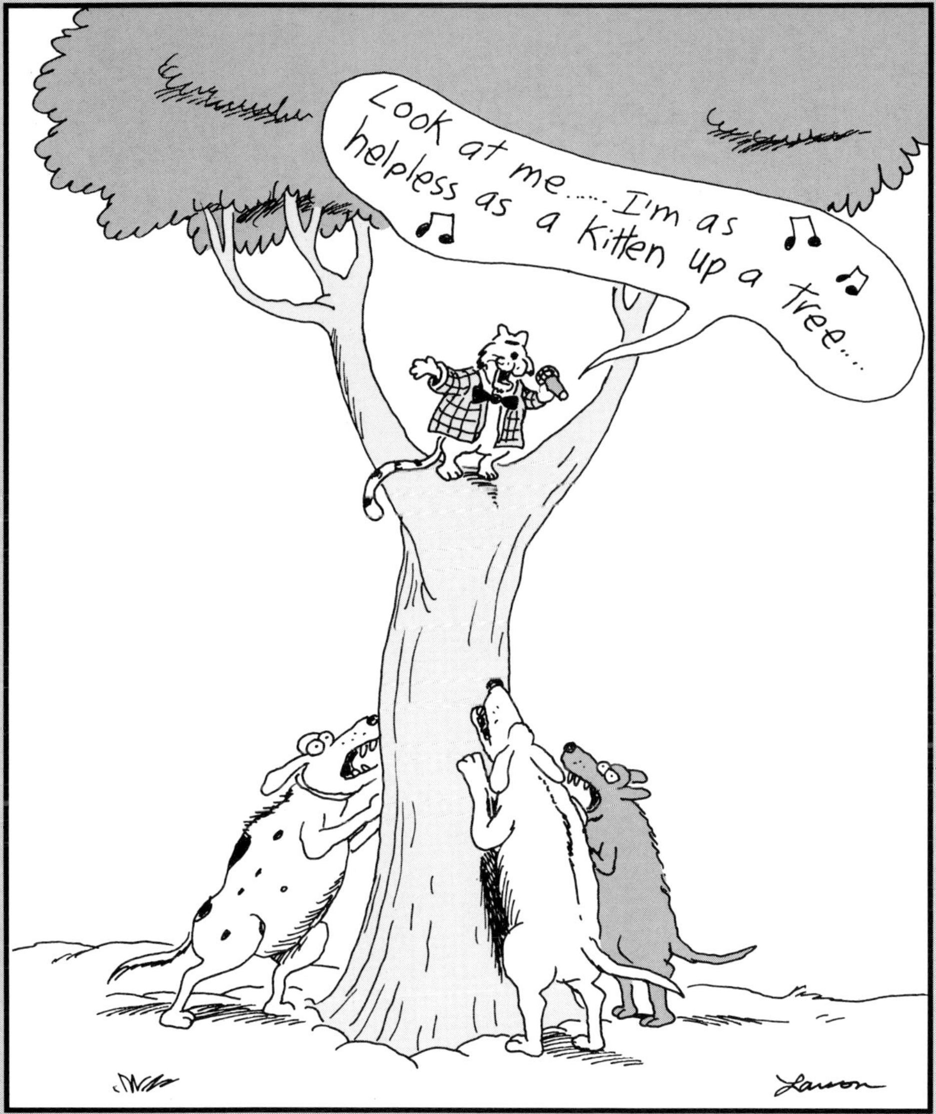
Look at me...... I'm as helpless as a kitten up a tree....
Larson

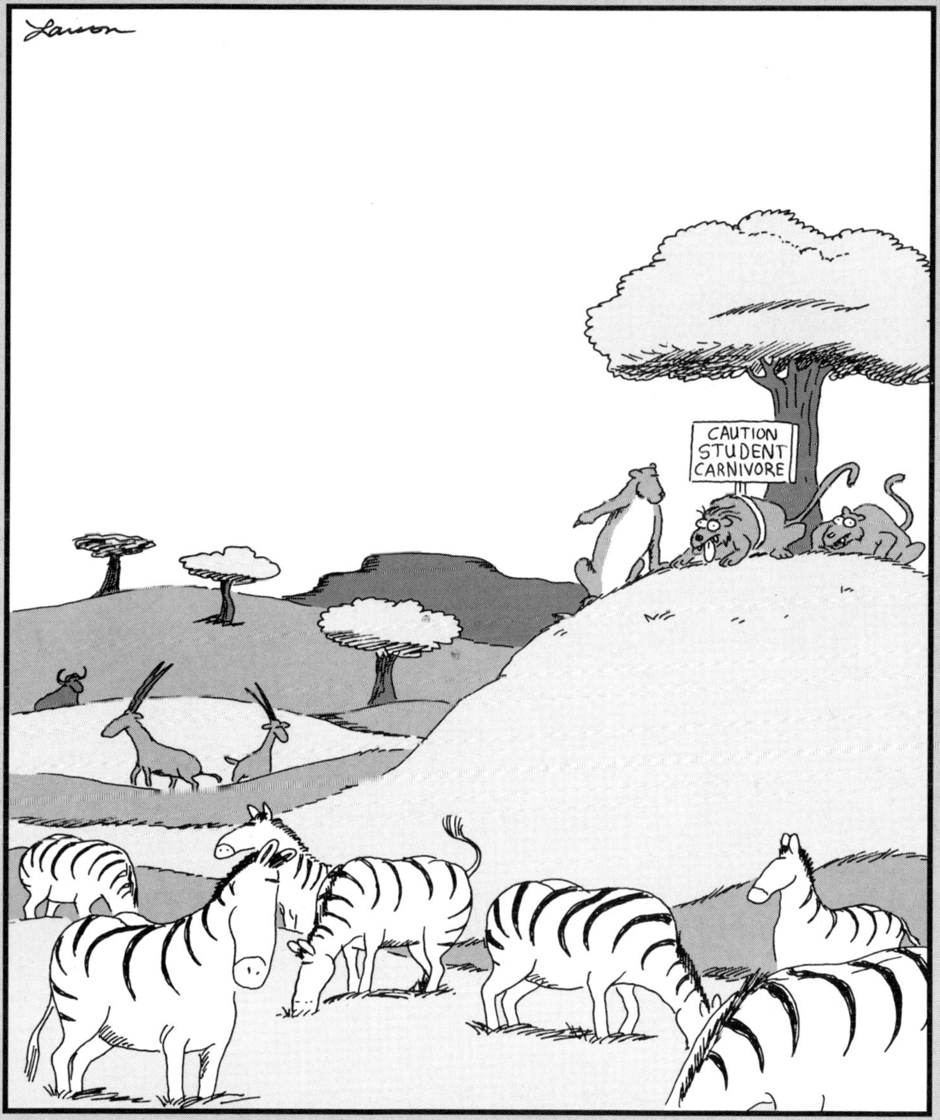
Larson
CAUTION
STUDENT
CARNIVORE

"Well, I seen all the commotion, with that there monster destroyin' half the city and whatnot, and I says to myself, 'Hell! Why don't someone just shoot the varmint?'"

Despite being well-financed by the tobacco industry, the newly formed Smokers' Mountaineering Club met its doom just a few moments after leaving base camp.

"You're new here, aincha, kid? Well, on some days the sandwiches contain a dead scorpion. ... Not *every* day, but *some* days—that's why it's hell, kid."

Afterword

I have one last thing to share with you. It's a true story. And one that reveals what I believe to be the seminal moment in my life when I discovered the wonder and magic of art.

One day, when I was about eight or nine years old, my dad called me over to the kitchen table and asked me to sit down next to him. With a sheet of paper under one hand and a pen in the other, he began to tell me a story. And as he spoke, he drew. Spellbound, I watched and listened.

This, then, in my dad's own words (or as best as I can recall), is the story he imparted to me on that fateful day. But beware-- the faint-of-heart should consider going no further.

Here's Dad:

So there's this teacher, and one day she asks a little kid in her grade-school class to go up to the blackboard and draw something. "Doesn't matter what -- just anything," she explains. "And afterwards," she says, now addressing the rest of the class, "I want all of you-- one by one-- to go up to the blackboard and add something to the <u>same</u> drawing, each time creating something new."

And so the first kid walks up to the blackboard, takes the chalk, and draws this:

and says, "That's a box."

Then the next kid goes up to the blackboard, adds a few lines, and says,

"That's a football field."

And then the next kid walks up to the blackboard, draws this:

and says, "That's a music stand."
Are you following this, Gary? [My dad knew from experience it was always good to ask this question.]

And so then the next kid goes up, adds a line to the music stand, and says:

"That's a lightbulb."

Finally, the <u>last</u> little kid (it was a small class) walks up to the blackboard, draws some lines, steps back and says...

"That's my mom putting on her girdle."

[For the full effect, flip this page over -- just
like my dad did for me.]

Yes, not unlike my friends' parents who
were dragging them to museums, flashing multiplication
cards in their faces, and driving them to piano lessons,
my dad was no bystander when it came to his
own kid's development.*

-GL

* Someday I'll share with you his well-honed method of wearing
a long, black coat, pulling a nylon stocking over his head, holding a
flashlight under his chin, and with all the lights turned out, floating
through the house like a living corpse. Oh, the memories.